Lepidoptera II:
Portraits Of My
Colorful Flying Friends.

A Coloring Book Celebrating Our Natural World

F. Scott Crawford

Lepidoptera II: Portraits Of My Colorful Flying Friends.

A Coloring Book Celebrating Our Natural World

F. Scott Crawford

Published by:

Black Rock Publishing
3661 Stockton Drive
Carrollton, Texas 75010

This is **Volume II** of my **"Lepidoptera"** coloring books. This volume presents a series of recent watercolor style illustrations, two each for 14 different butterflies and moths, drawn by "spline-x" ~ Fotolia.com, reproduced under license from Fotolia; these were adapted to make line art which you can fill in with color. The first illustration is complete, and the second is partially completed, so you can see the sequence of work in creating the illustrations and get a better idea of the coloring process for the examples.

This coloring book provides two coloring pages for each guiding line illustration, so you can color in the natural colors from the original illustrations, and then you also have an extra page so you can try your hand at whatever color combinations strike your fancy for each butterfly or moth in the series.

These watercolor illustrations show a selection of butterflies and moths which matches up very closely to many of those butterfly and moth specimens which were in my personal butterfly collection assembled as a teenager in Oregon and Florida.

Produced in the United States of America.

ISBN-10: 1-51862-364-6

ISBN-13: 978-1518623646

DEDICATION:

For Maggie, "Forever & forever."

LET'S CELEBRATE YOUR OWN COLORFUL WORLD:

Use the colors that seem best to you.

"Stay in the lines" except when you have to go outside the lines to satisfy your artistic instincts and expand your horizons.

Relax. Concentrate. Use your feelings. Enjoy your creative impulses.

Lift your spirits. Take flight with your fantasy. Soar above it all.

Note: There are two pages for your colored drawings of each butterfly or moth in the series. This way, with the extra page you can first try your hand at natural colors ... and then do it again with whatever fantasy colors you like.

Inachis Io

Numphalis Antiopa

Colias Erate

Saturnia pavonia

Catocala Fraxini

Urania Leilus

Papillo machaon

Parnassius apollonius

Polygonia c-album

Troganoptera brookina

Morpho Anaxibia

Heliconius

Papilio Demodocus

Iphiclides podalirius

Papillo machaon

Troganoptera brookina

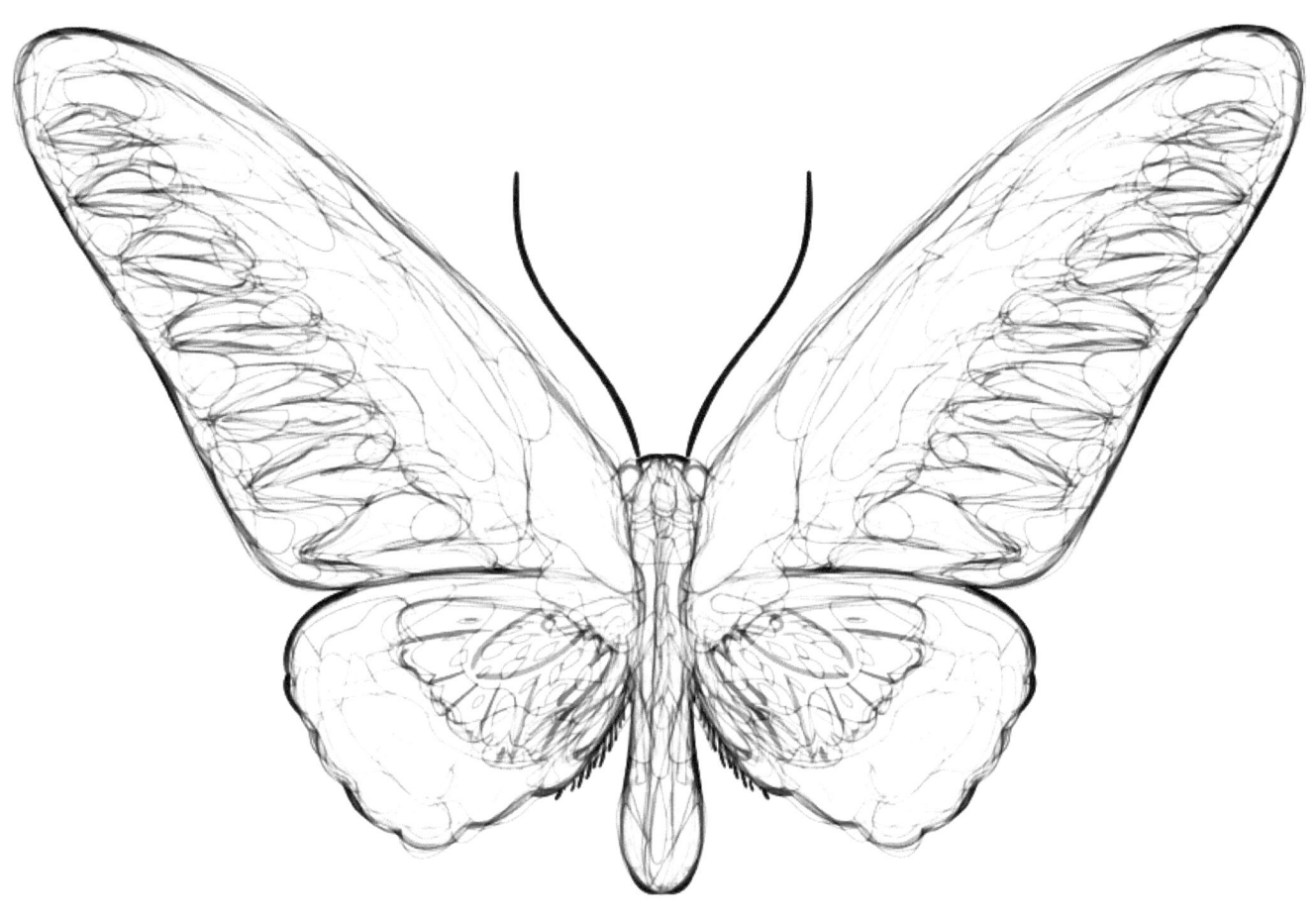

Saturnia pavonia

Urania Leilus

Morpho Anaxibia

Numphalis Antiopa

Inachis Io

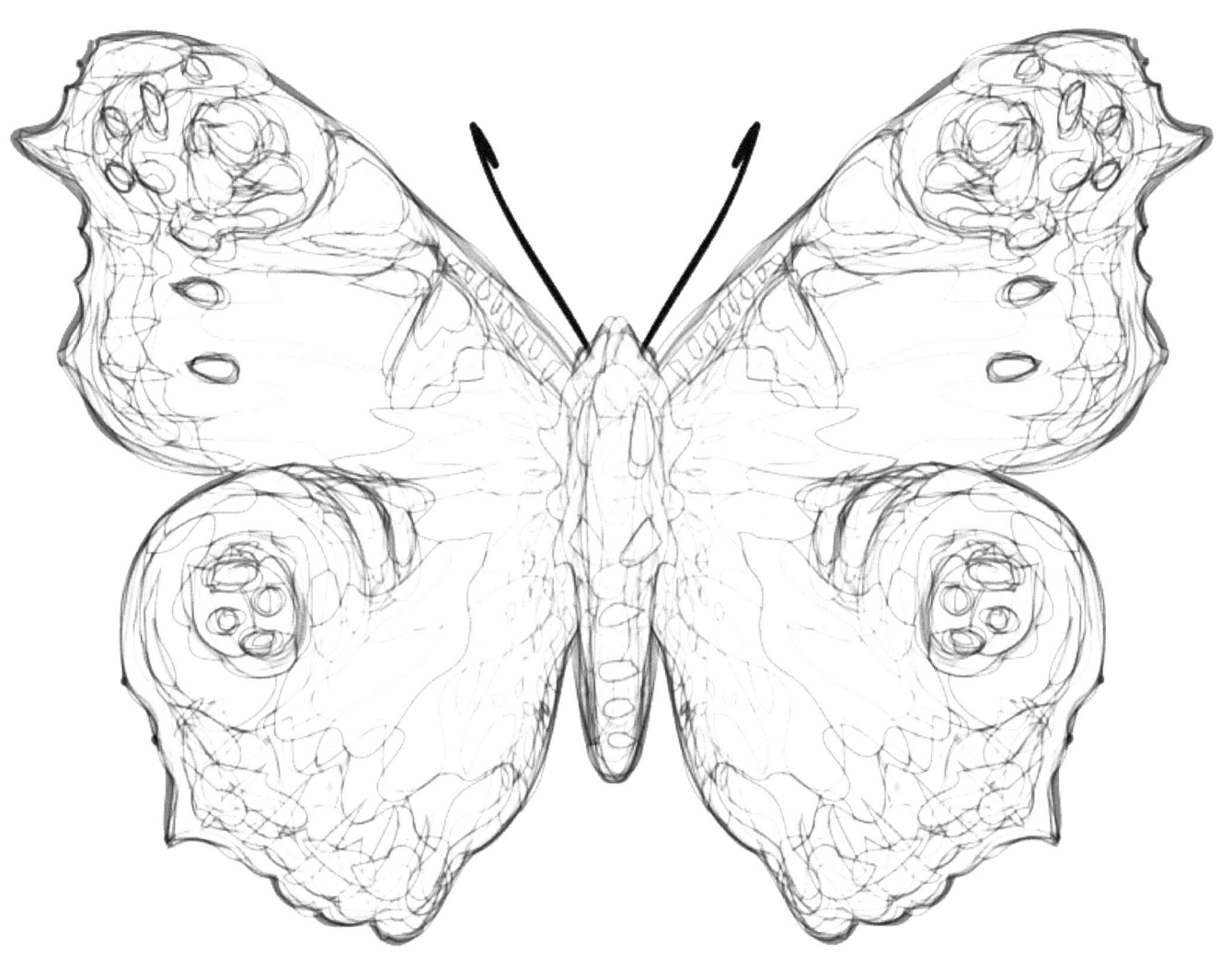

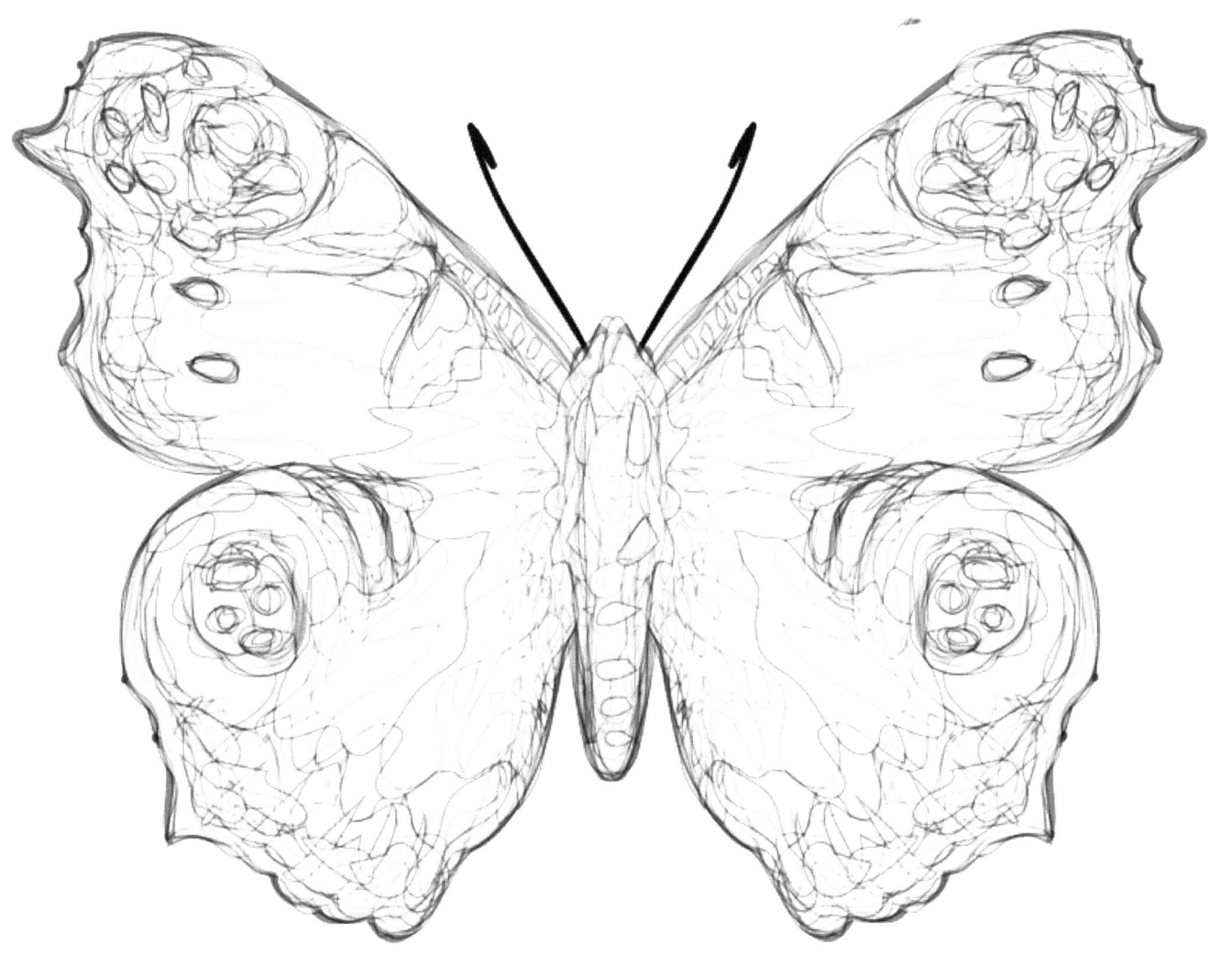

Parnassius apollonius

Catocala Fraxini

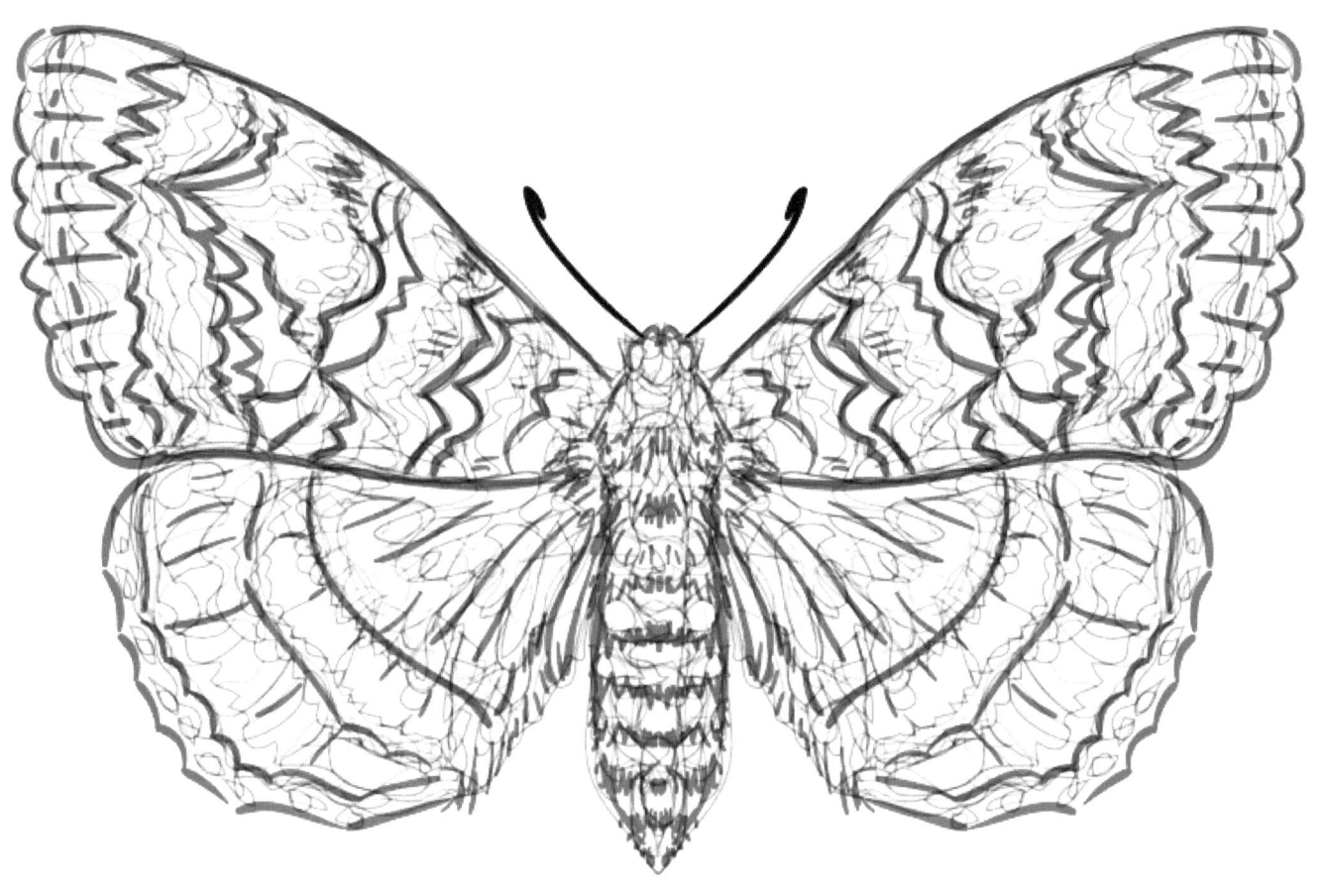

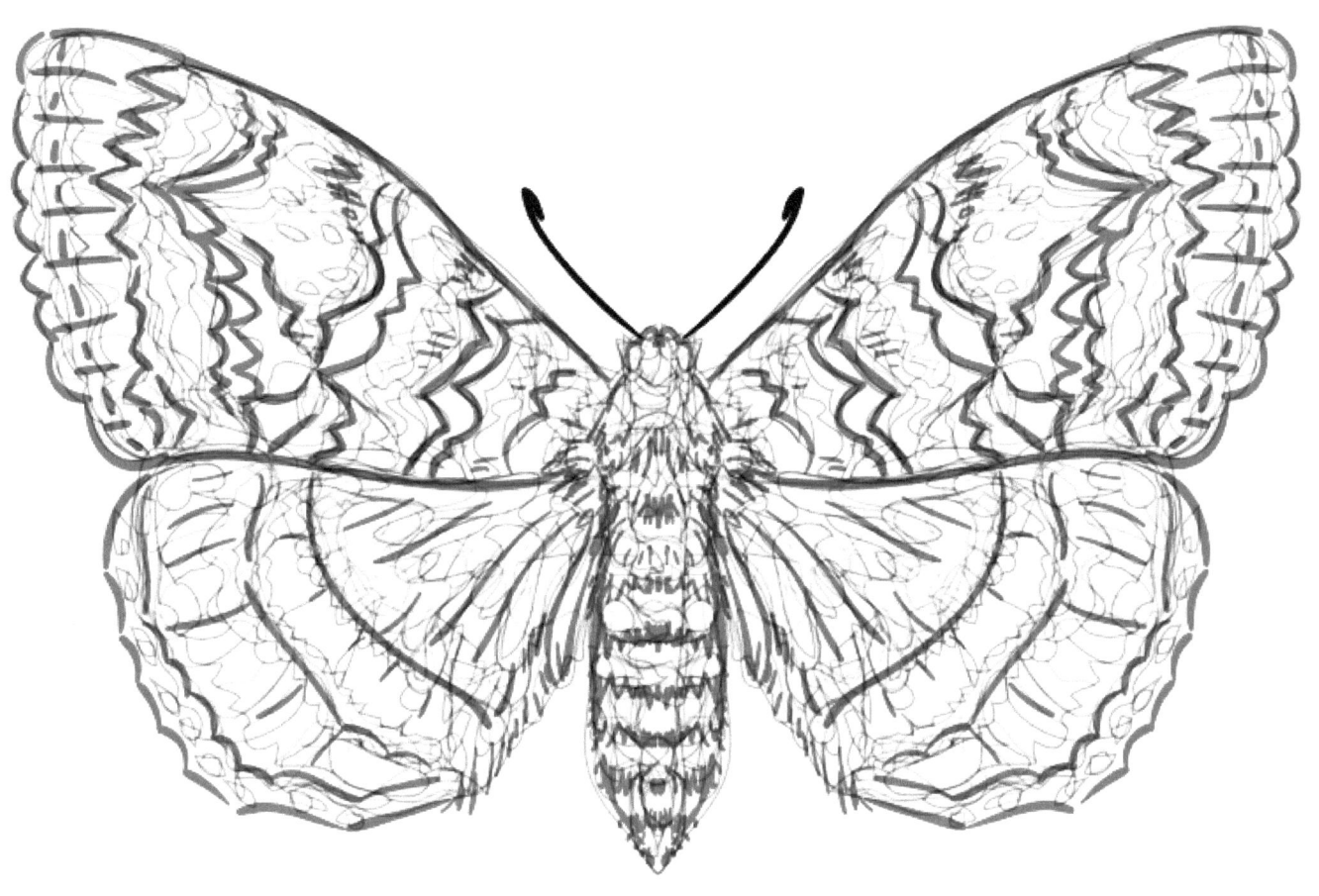

Colias Erate

Heliconius

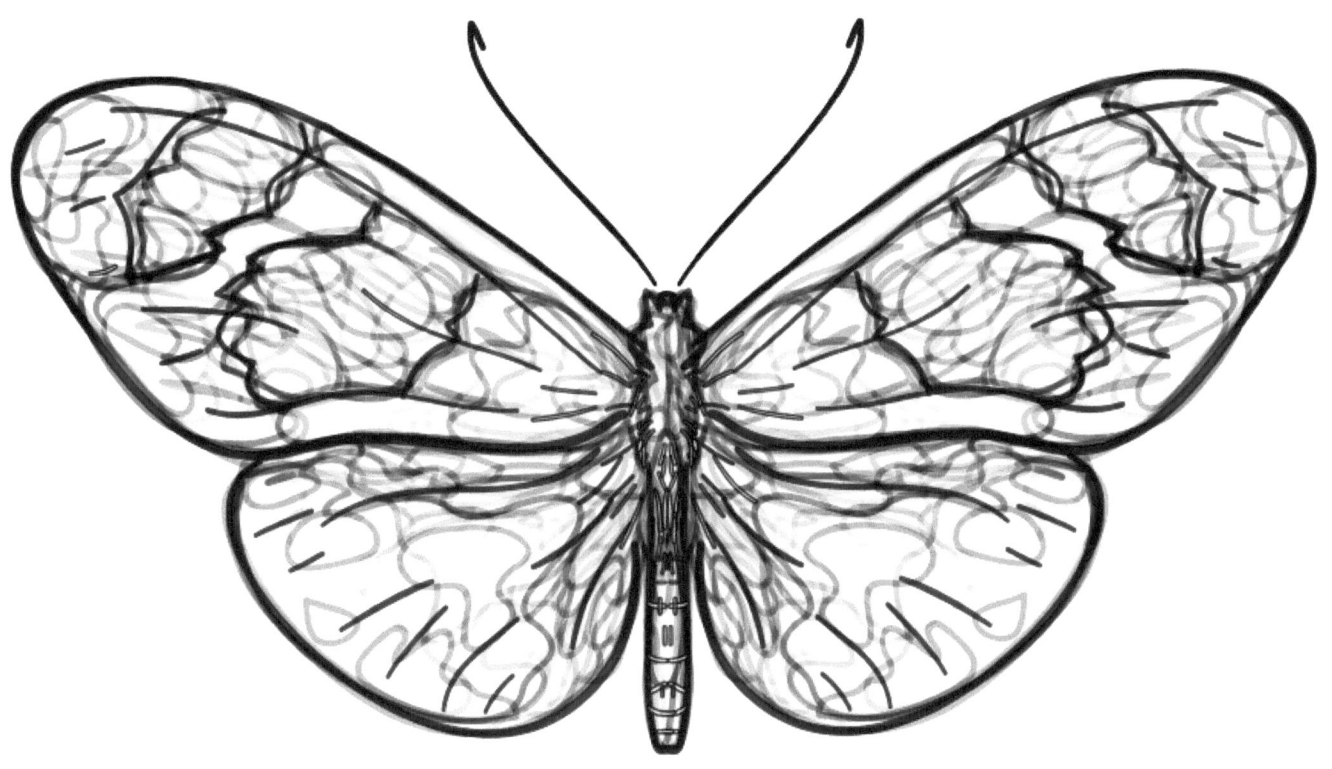

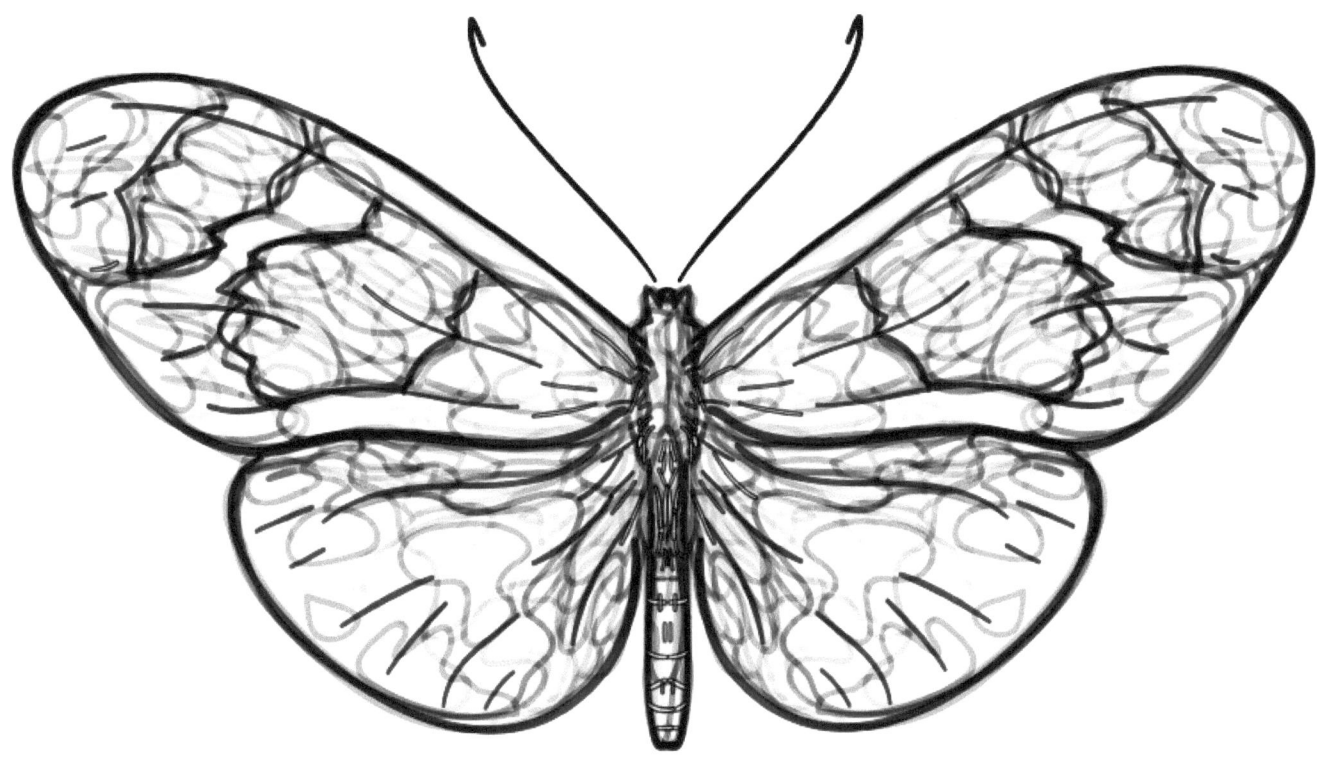

Polygonia c-album

Papilio Demodocus

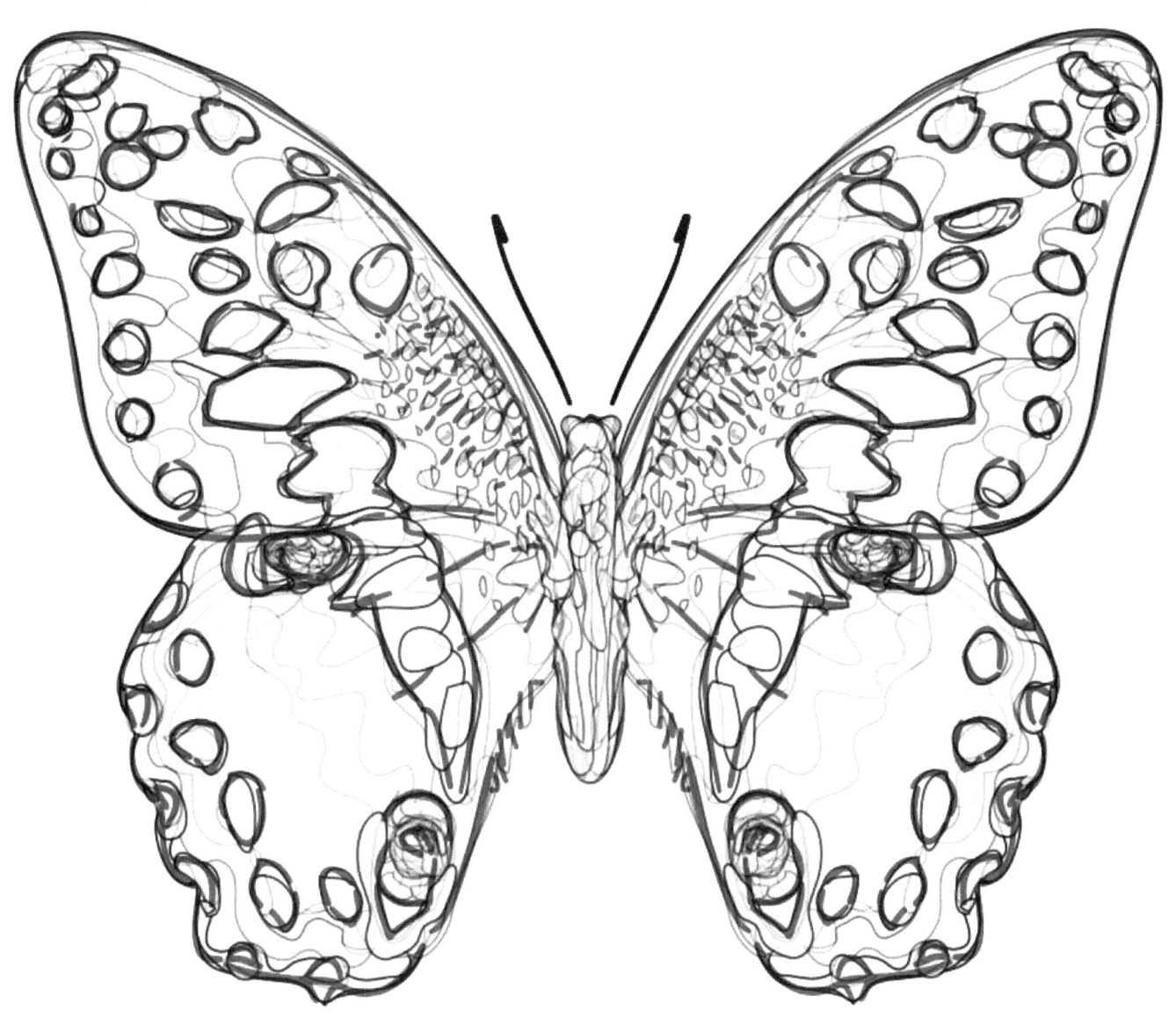

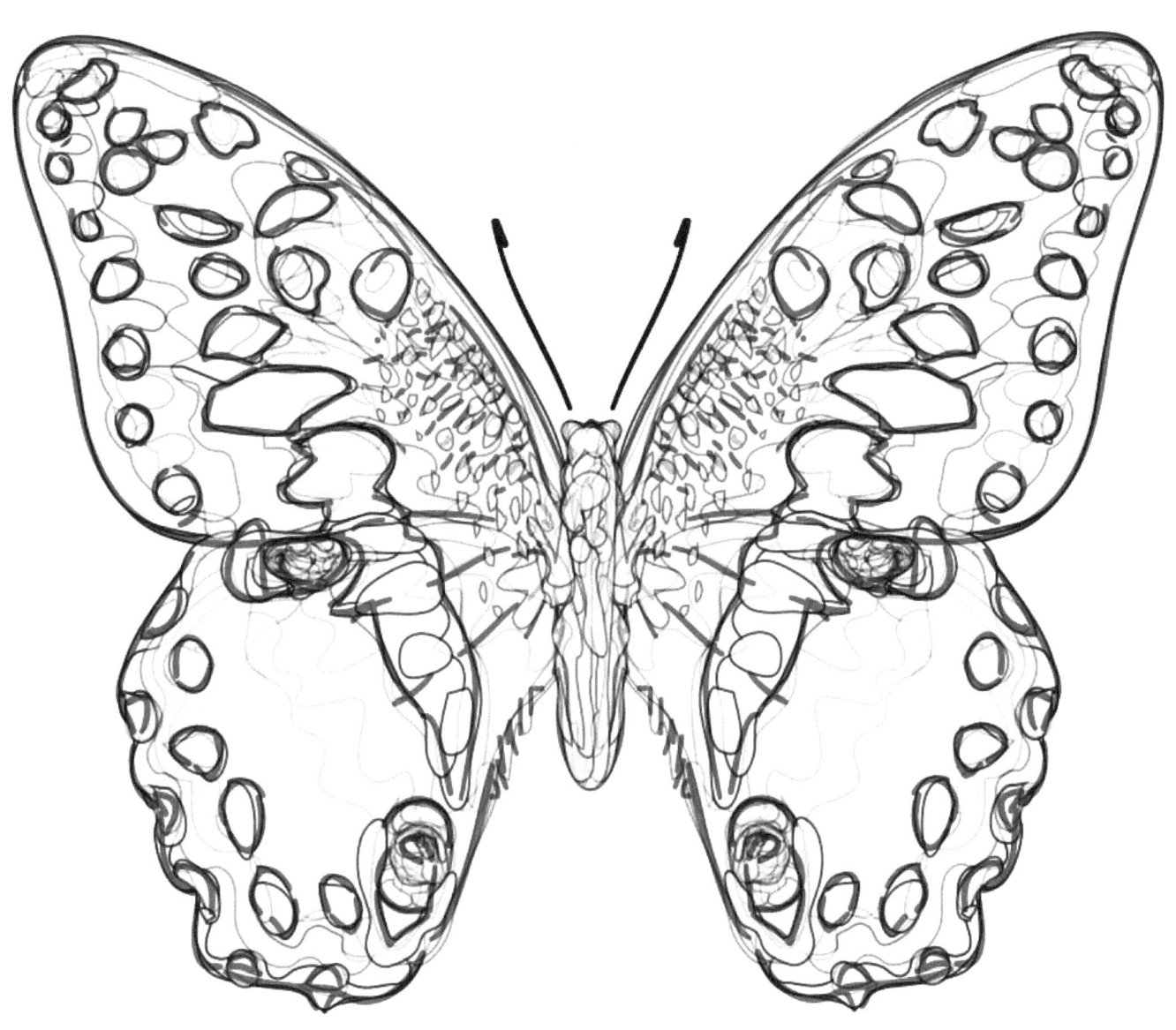

Iphiclides podalirius

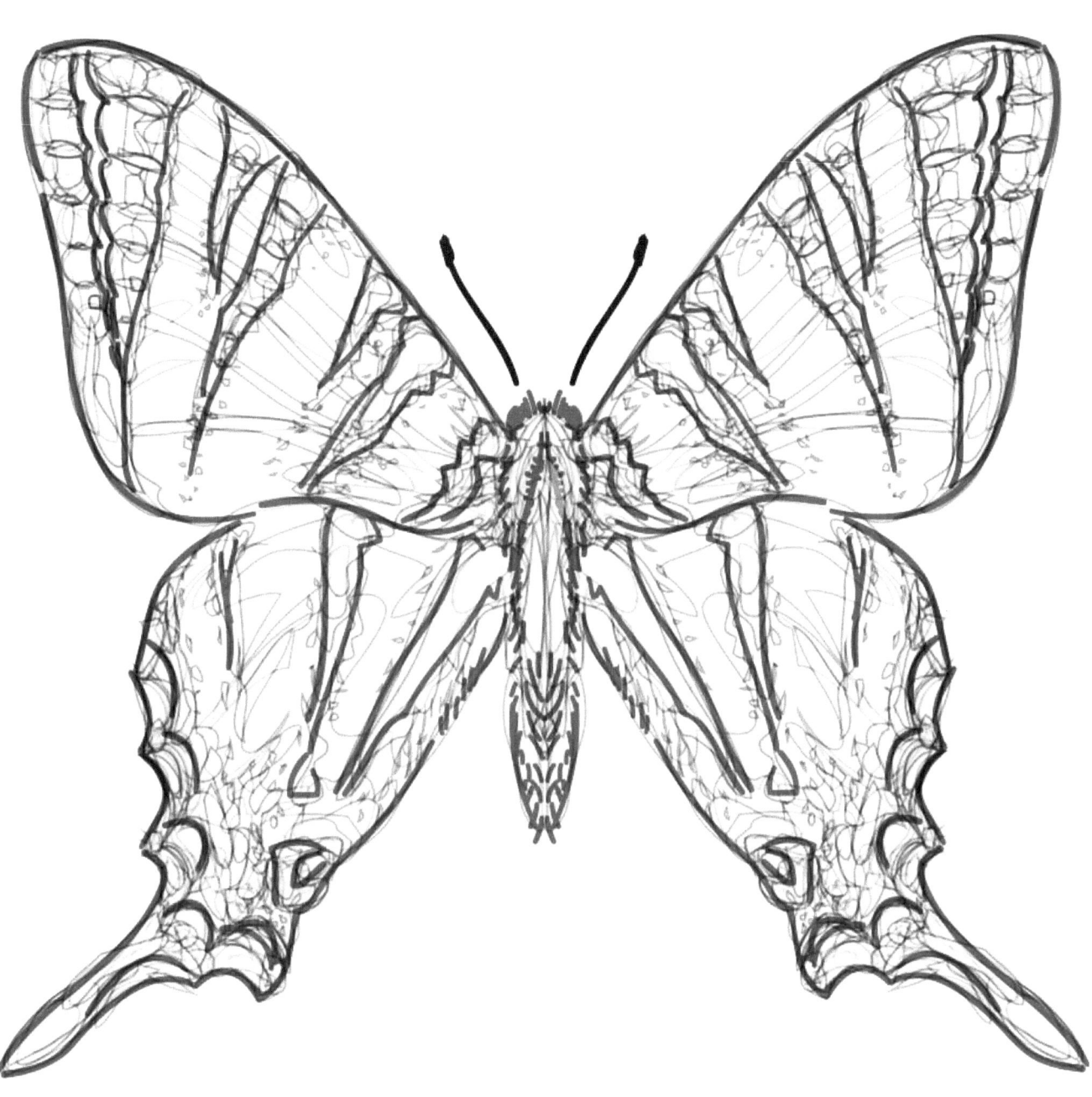

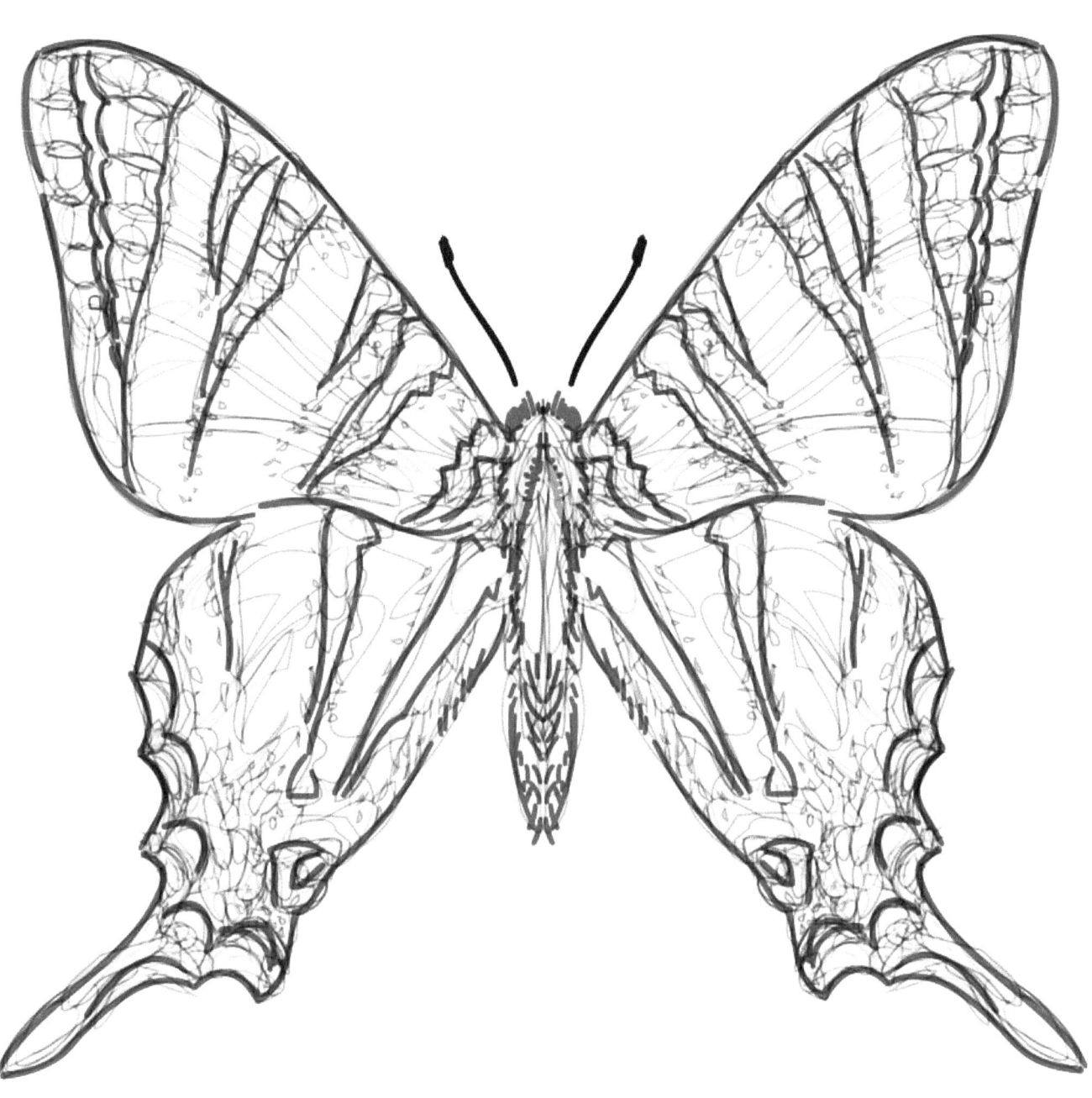